Herbert and Jeanne McGonigle

Our Story

Herbert Boyd McGonigle

MA, BD, DD, PHD

British Library Cataloguing in Publication Data.
A catalogue record for this book is available from the British Library

ISBN 978 0 86071 769 0

A Commissioned Publication Printed by

MOORLEYS
Print, Design & Publishing
info@moorleys.co.uk · www.moorleys.co.uk

OUR DEDICATION

My lovely Jeanne was taken from us at 7am on Sunday, 5th February, 2017. Our hearts are lonely without her presence and every day I look on the photograph where she smiles down on us from the piano. She was with me fifty-five years and six months and in all that time she was loving, kind and generous to me and to her sons, Keith, Stephen, Jonathan, and to her grandchildren, Joe and her darling Lucy. But we continue in faith, knowing that we shall meet again when the Lord shall sound the trumpet and the dead in Christ shall rise first.

Herbert and Jeanne McGonigle
Our Story

My grandfather, Joseph McGonigle, was born in 1865 and he was the son of James McGonigle who also was a farmer. He married in 1885 to a lady called Eliza Adams and they settled down in Mullinahose, Ballybofey, Co. Donegal. My father, Joseph McGonigle, was born in 1892 and was married to Lucy Quinton in 1921 and there were six children. The eldest was Mary (1922), Harry (1924), Lydia (1926), Jean (1928) and Joe (1930). I was born on 15th August, 1939, the last of six children. My grandfather was alive at that time and he took me with him walking around the farm. I have little information about grandad but I knew he was a believer and read his bible every day. He used a piece of paper to mark the spot where he had finished and long after he was gone, the paper remained. He didn't tell his family that he was up before the courts in 1908 and was fined. The record shows him at court and the following is proof that he was to blame.

> Petty Sessions Order Books, Defendant, Joseph McGonigle, 6 May, 1908, Court at Stranorlar, Co. Donegal. Admits offence of possession of an unlicensed dog on 5 May 1908. Complainant: M. Fallon, Ballybofey, Sergeant Royal Irish Constabulary; Defendant: Joseph McGonigle, Mullinahose, parish of Stranorlar. Names of Witnesses, etc. Defendant Admits Offence. Cause of Complaint: Unlicensed Dog: The Defendant on the 5th day of May 1908 at Mullinahose in said County unlawfully had in his possession one dog not fully licensed. Defendant convicted: To pay for one penny for costs and sixpence forthwith and in default of payment to be imprisoned in the Gaol at Londonderry for seven days with hard labour unless said sums be sooner paid & to take out licence forthwith.

I am sure that my granddad didn't tell his family! Our granddad was alive and welcomed all the children; he was interested in the fields and took me to see the family at work. Then came the end in 1946 and we buried him in Stranorlar Church of Ireland and later on I knew the grave where he was buried. All the family were Church of Ireland and all attended Stranorlar, next door to Ballybofey. My father farmed the land and I recall horses, cows, hens, duck, geese, etc. My family belonged to the Church and in the twenty-six counties, Roman Catholics made up to ninety-five per cent. When I was young, Catholics and Protestants got on well and I never remember any division.

When I was six I was enrolled in Dooish National School and in five years I was trained in mathematics, English, and in the Irish language. All of southern Ireland were taught the Irish language and in this subject I was doing well. We were taught in Irish and trained in that subject and to read books in Irish. All my brothers and sisters were gone and at work and the girls trained in nursing. There were seven Protestants in our classes and that was out of forty students. Twice a week Protestants got a half an hour to play while the Catholics were doing Mass.

Joseph McGonigle's farm in Co. Donegal
where his son Herbert was born 15 August 1939

My uncle, Herbert Quinton, visited us at home and the conversation was always about moving into the North. When I was eleven, my parents sold the farm to a neighbour and I was finished at Dooish School. I remember the day well when the farm was sold and Herbert Quinton, my father and mother and me headed out for the North. We crossed the border at Pettigo and an hour later we had landed at Whitehill North, Irvinestown, Co. Fermanagh. It was about forty-five miles and all Fermanagh looked the same as we left southern Ireland. People gathered to welcome us and we were busy getting the place going to suit us. The schools were for Protestants and Catholics but at that juncture there was no problem in religion. Irish was not taught in Protestant schools and before long I was left with a grammar but I can still remember Irish words! We joined the Church of Ireland and next door was the Protestant school. I joined it at eleven and stayed there for five years. These were good years and I studied my lessons and made good progress. Then at fifteen years I was finished and the Technical College in Enniskillen was open. I studied and was accepted and from Monday to Friday I attended there, eleven miles from home.

Joseph McGonigle with his wife, Lucy McGonigle nee Quinton

McGonigle family farmhouse from 1951 in Whitehill North, Co. Fermanagh

When I reached home that afternoon, my father and mother told me about a fortnight mission that was to take place in Lisnarick about a mile away. Mr Bill McClintock. was going round the farms telling them of the mission and inviting people to come. My mother was eager to go but my father and I held back to see what would happen. My mother went and was really converted and came home with joy to tell us what had happened. Then I made up my mind to go the second Sunday and when I got there, everything was strange. There were about forty people and I knew some of them. Bill McClintock was in charge and he preached in every service. Choruses were introduced and that was the first time I had choruses and hymns. It was all very strange but I liked Bill McClintock and he was very friendly. As the second week went on I grew very anxious and on Friday night I was saved! Then on the final Sunday night my father gave his heart to the Lord. My mother was overjoyed and she promised Mr McClintock that from now on, this house would be a place of prayer.

Mr. McClintock started a meeting every month in the hall and we all went. Then I discovered Manoo Mission Hall, about three miles away and I started attending. There I met Mr. and Mrs. Loane, Mr. and Mrs. Irvine, Mr. Jim Simpson and many other good people. While attending Manoo Mission Hall, the Revd. Keys knew about us and summoned my mother and myself into the vestry. He gave us a very strong lecture and warned us about going back. Finally my parents withdrew and started going to the Methodist Church in Irvinestown. There we met the Revd. Edwards and he was an evangelical and welcomed us gladly. There was a prayer meeting in the home of Mr. and Mrs. Irvine and one evening she brought two books and handed them to me. They were by John Wesley; *Forty-four Sermons,* and, *A Plain Account of Christian Perfection.* I took them home and read them closely and I discovered that John Wesley believed the same as I did! A few years afterwards I was in their home and I mentioned to them that they were the first two books that ever I owned. Now they sit proudly on my shelves.

In the course of a few years, what I heard in the Methodist Church and from Christians, I was deeply convinced that my heart was not right and on the Easter Monday in Manoo Hall, I was filled with the Holy

Spirit. That was sixty three years ago and down through the years I have never lost what God did for me on Easter Monday.

Mr. McClintock told us about the Killadeas Camp Meeting that was going on every July meeting, from Sunday to Sunday and invited us to come. I shall never forget that meeting with 700 in attendance and what a service. The Revd. Len Ravenhill was the preacher in 1953 and what a meeting! Crowds attended every meeting and prayer meetings were held every day of the services. In subsequent years I was privileged to hear Revd. Maynard James, Revd. Duncan Campbell, Revd. W.P. Nicholson, Major Alistair Smith, Dr. and Mrs. Colin Peckham, Dr. Sydney Martin, Dr. Dale Yocum, Revd. John Harris, Revd. Sam Ennis, and many more outstanding preachers. The final night was the climax and hundreds of people stood listening. I attended from 1955 until 2007 and I have never been in Conventions like Killadeas.

Going back to my studies at Enniskillen Technical College, I learned a lot there and one year before I finished, I was presented with the Cup that is given to the best all-round student. I was thrilled at the Cup and it sat in my living room for a whole year. The Technical College closed in June and I was looking at Bible Colleges. On the first of January 1957 Bill McClintock came to visit us in the company of Revd. J. B. Maclagen, a Scottish preacher from Glasgow and now a District Superintendent on the South District. He was over to preach at New Year meetings in Enniskillen and Mr. McClintock told him of me and my desire to find a college. He was very friendly and stopped about two hours and told us of Nazarene College in Glasgow. I was interested and he told me if I should write to the Principal, Revd. Dr. Hugh Rae, and tell him my position. Before he left he knelt down and prayed for my father and mother, my sisters and brothers, and said that God was going to visit all my family and that they would be saved. They left and my mother and father thought that he was a man of God and they had promised to pray for him.

In May I joined a coach going to Bundoran Convention, Co. Donegal, to attend meetings of the Bundoran Convention. Dr. Sydney Martin was there and he preached. I did not know that he was minister of Parkhead Nazarene Church, Glasgow, and I listened very closely. He preached from Genesis 32:28 and I remember his illustrations. He told the story of a soldier who was killed in battle and his picture was hung in the Royal Corps of Signals as he grasped both ends of the wire as he lay dying. It was entitled, *It Reached*. Not bad for sixty-one years! Dr. Martin became my favourite preacher and four months later I was sitting in his class in Church History in Hurlet Nazarene College, Paisley, Scotland.

Hurlet College housed twenty-one students and I was there for three years. I did well in Church History, Systematic Theology, Bible Introduction and Exegesis, Holiness, Apologetics, Pastoral Theology and Homiletics. Then after a year, we moved to the outskirts of Ashton-under-Lyne, near Manchester. It was the former College of Calvary Holiness Church which had been incorporated into the Church of the Nazarene in June 1955. We stayed two terms in Beech Lawn and then moved to our present position in Didsbury, Manchester. After the three years were up, I was surprised to receive numerous books as I was awarded the College's highest standard. The Revd. Dr. Hugh Rae was its Principal and all through the years and down until he died in 2009, he was my friend and mentor.

During the final term I was asked to go to Walthamstow Nazarene Church, London, and preached twice there. Then there was a letter from the Church's secretary to say that I was invited to pastor their Church. I arrived in London in the first week of August and settled in. I didn't know the Church but I familiarized my memory of about thirty members. I got round all Church members and I was gratified to learn that they were all Nazarenes and prayer time of a Tuesday were times of rich blessing. The capital of England surprised me after having been brought up in Irvinestown! There were about ten million in London and thousands didn't go Church.

Then I met Jeanne! She was a widow living in Leyton and worshipping at the Elim Church. Jeanne and Pamela were the children of Charles and Edith Lait and used to go sometimes to the Church of England. When Jeanne was about eleven the family heard about George Jeffries and went to hear him. The gospel was fully preached and the four of them were saved. They started attending the Assemblies of God and grew mightily in grace. Jeanne attended the Elim Church and when she was twenty-one, she married Cyril Romig. They had a son, Keith, born to them in 1946 and Cyril died in 1951. Jeanne was worshipping in the Elim Church, Leyton, and Keith was with her. I got to know her and before very long we were in love. The next year, in September 1961, we were married in the Elim Church in Leyton. A week was spent in Herstmonceux in Sussex and we returned to live in Liverpool Road. We both worked and then Jeanne

Charles and Edith Lait

was expecting and on August 25, 1962, our son, Stephen Wesley, was born. The three of us loved Stephen and he was brought up in the faith. Then our son Jonathan was born on the March 23, 1965. We were proud to show off our boys and Stephen and Jonathan grew in the Lord.

We enjoyed the Walthamstow Church and the people there were so kind and generous. In 1963 we were invited to hold a revival with the Revd. Maynard James. He was known to me because I had met him and I was delighted that he accepted. He came and preached and our church was full and many could not get in. I often talked with him about the *Flame*, a bimonthly magazine that went round the churches. He told me there was a vacancy and he asked me to write the *Children's Page*. I had not written before but I stuck at it and it lasted four years. Mr. James became my friend and it lasted while he was living. From 1963 until his death in 1988, I accompanied him to campaigns and to Conventions.

In January 1965 a letter came asking me to preach at Uddingston Nazarene Church, six miles south of Glasgow. I went to Uddingston and preached and just a little later there came the invitation to go there and pastor. Jeanne was not sure if I should go but eventually we were prepared for going and said farewell to the congregation. By this time the church was thriving and the people did not want us to go. Jonathan was only two months old but eventually we went. Uddingston was one of the first places to hold a Nazarene Church in Scotland and I was following the Revd. Jock Henson, a man of God. We really enjoyed pastoring the church and getting to know the people. In 1967 I was elected as President of the Nazarene Young People's Society and in 1968 I attended the General Assembly in Kansas City, Missouri, USA. It opened my eyes to see the church in all its strength and I had three months of missions in many churches.

My vehicle at that time was a twelve-seater minibus and we used it for gathering children on Sunday. When we went to Whitehill North, Irvinestown, there was room for my father and mother and we took them all over the place. My father loved the minibus and thought he could sit in it for hours. I remember one holiday when we set out for Londonderry and we packed up the stove and kettle and started quite early. The sun was shining all through the day and my parents were delighted to come with us. My father and mother didn't get many outings and they wanted to see Londonderry. We stopped at Sion Mills, Co. Tyrone, and walked round the shops. My Dad was delighted and we showed him round the town. We then headed for Strabane, Co. Tyrone, and did the tour of the town. A while before when we lived in Mullinahose, Co. Donegal, I remember Mary, Harry and Joe shopping in Strabane and I thought of it miles away. Now my parents walked around Strabane and thought it marvellous. Finally we reached Londonderry and we stopped outside it and ate our sandwiches. The day was beautiful and we enjoyed our lunch. Finally we made Londonderry and there were many things we looked at as we walked round the city. Londonderry is a walled city and we remembered the time that Protestants were shut up in the city and the Revd. Dr. George Walker, Anglican vicar of the city, in 1690, made himself captain and rallied the Protestants and gave fight to its rebels. Dr. Walker eventually won the day and a ship got through and they were saved. Afterwards a monument was raised to Dr. Walker and he looks proudly over the city. Now it was 1974 and soldiers were there guarding the place. Stephen and Jonathan and myself walked the walls and were interested in everything. Finally we left and motored back to Whitehill North. My father and mother were overjoyed and my father said he would go again tomorrow!

The next year we were back and we all decided upon the south of Ireland and planned to go to Standhill in Sligo. We crossed the border at Belcoo and were on the road, N16, to Manorhamilton. The weather was fine and all the way to Manorhamilton the scenery was beautiful. We went round the town of Manorhamilton and soon on to Sligo. We visited the shops and stores and then onto R292 to Strandhill on the coast. We took the road up to the top and were delighted with the scenery. Before us was Sligo Bay and as far as we could tell Coney Island was magnificent. We stayed there all day and the air was lovely. My parents loved it and we spent the day in glorious sunshine. Neither Dad nor Mum had been there before and it was lovely. We cooked our meals before we left home and it was so good to eat and enjoy all the scenery. We stayed there until about six o'clock and then motored home in the minibus. We talked all about it on the way home and it was so refreshing to see all the countryside so green and lovely.

Our two sons were doing well at school and after six years in Uddingston Church, we came to pastor the Leeds Dewsbury Road. This was new territory to Jeanne but we soon settled in and had large congregations both morning and evening. The evening congregation was the largest and the church was packed every Sunday night. After a campaign with the Revd. Maynard James, when people came from near and far, the church was full and we started looking for new premises. While at Leeds I finished my BD degree at London University and then took up my MA works at Leeds University. Jeanne and I enjoyed pastoring and we reckoned that we had many years to stay in Leeds. I was invited to teach at British Isles Nazarene College and went over every Thursday morning. I enjoyed the visits and I was given exegesis on New Testament books.

A few months before graduating, the Principal, the Revd. Hugh Rae and Mrs. Rae, arrived at our house. It wasn't long before Dr. Rae brought up the subject – would I be interested in coming to the College full time? Dr. Rae offered us a full-time lectureship and he said that Church History, Wesley Studies and Homiletics were our portion if we would go. Right up to that moment we hadn't thought of moving and with our very full church we were happy and content with our calling. I cannot recall a time when Jeanne and I were in such a quandary. Our people wanted us to stay and we did not want to break the Lord's anointing upon us. We were *very happy* to stay in Leeds and I wanted to know what the will of God was for us. Together Jeanne and I decided to pray one from another and eventually we had the answer – to go to the college. At that time Mr. Geoff Clarkson was the Church Secretary and before the service, I told him we were leaving. Geoff looked at me, unable to speak. When the morning service was over, I said that Geoff had something to say. He announced that we were leaving and had the honour of a church that felt blessed just after five years. The people were stunned and at the door many people were asking Jeanne and I to stay. That Sunday morning leaves a visible impression on my heart and after forty-two years, that morning will last for ever.

We left in September 1976 and landed at this house on the Monday. Dr. and Mrs. Rae had lived in this house and had moved out. We settled down and Stephen and Jonathan went to school. For ten years I was in charge of Church History, Wesley Studies and Homiletics. For me the clock had moved round in a circle and we were back in study in our own College. I revelled in my lectures and for that ten year period, Dr. Rae was Principal. We couldn't tell how wonderful Dr. Rae was in charge those years and I am always grateful for the period when we were on the staff.

In September 1980 my father was taken ill and I phoned home each night and on the September 21, our Dad was taken home to heaven. I immediately flew home and it was great to see Mother bearing up. The funeral normally takes place on the third day and it was marvellous to see the home filled with people, both Protestant and Catholic. Mr. Bill McClintock was in charge and he told the people that it was in 1955 that my Dad gave his heart to the Lord. The home was packed and outside there was a crush to see all that happened. All my brothers and sisters were there and it was cheering to see all the people that had come to pay their respects to our Dad. More people were at the graveyard and we buried our Dad in certain hope of the Resurrection of the dead. It was at the Lisnarick Mission Hall in 1955 that all three of us, Mother, Father and I gave our hearts to the Lord and now, and now, twenty-five years later, in that packed churchyard, we said our farewell to my Dad. I had loved him all my live and now our Mother went on living there until it was time to go.

In the spring of 1983, Dr. Tom Schofield took up the Regional Director and the District Assembly was held. There was a good deal of arguing who the next District Superintendant should be and I went to the Assembly intending to vote for the Revd. Len McNeil. The first ballot was announced that Herbert McGonigle was leading by thirty votes! I was stunned by the announcement and I got hold of Dr. Rae and asked him what I should do. Dr. Rae was very kind and asked me if I was willing to take up the District Superintendency. I said yes, hoping that my name would drop to the bottom. A second ballot was taken and I was just a few votes short. A third was taken and I was elected. I carried on my college work until the break in June and being District Superintendent I was busy all the time. The time was passing by and I made journeys to the churches and held elections to see twelve of our churches filled.

Then from December I began to wonder if my job suited me. Early in January I wrote to the General Superintendent to say that I would not be standing at our District Assembly. I resigned and Dr. Rae said that there was a vacancy in the college and they were happy to see me back. A year in District Superintendency taught me many things and I was glad to be back in the college.

Then in 1988 Dr. and Mrs. Rae retired and I was approached about being Principal. That was in January 1988 and travelling to a week-end at the Carrickfergus Church in Antrim, the prayer was answered and I was elected Principal. I took up PhD studies in 1990 at the University of Keele, Staffordshire, in Wesley Studies. Dr. Bill Parkes had told me that there was a professor in Keele that was also interested in Wesley studies. I wrote to him and asked him if I might visit. I went down and met Professor John H.Y. Briggs, MA, FSA, FRHistS. He was so kind to me and we settled on the subject, *Sufficient Saving Grace: John Wesley's Evangelical Arminianism.* I valued meeting Professor Briggs at regular intervals and he was always ready to go over the whole period of Wesley's itinerant evangelism. There was quite a lot to do in this examination and I got it finished before the time. Professor Briggs invited Dr. John Walsh, Emeritus Fellow, Jesus College, Oxford, and Dr. Alan P. F. Sell. In May 1994 Jeanne and I travelled to the University of Keele and I was awarded the degree of Doctor of Philosophy.

Right in the middle of writing my thesis, Dr. John Bowling invited Jeanne and myself to Olivet Nazarene University to offer the degree of Doctor of Divinity. Jeanne hadn't been on a plane before and she was frightened. At that time we were worshipping in Salford Church of the Nazarene and Frank and May Williamson were very interested in our going to Olivet. He took Jeanne aside and pointed out that with prayer and encouragement Jeanne would be able to go. We reached Manchester and boarded the plane and from that date she would travel with me. When we reached Chicago John and Jill were waiting for us and the meeting was a part of long friendship. We stayed at the University and preached at various intervals. Then on Saturday, May 9, 1992, I spoke to three thousand students and faculty and they donned me in a gown, hood and cap. It was a memorable day and I will ever thank John and Jill for giving me the invitation to preach.

Jeanne and I had always treasured a week or so away and we looked forward to going on holiday. Then there was a letter from Cornwall written by Mr. William Burton. He had obviously read the *Flame* and mentioned to me that he was interested in what I wrote and invited Jeanne and myself to Quenchwell Methodist Church in Cornwall. We had never visited Cornwall before and having written and accepted it, we looked forward to August. On Wednesday, August 7, 1985 we set out wondering what the venture would hold and travelled down the M1 to Birmingham and then branched off on the M5 and travelled to Exeter and then on the A30 right down to Scorrier. We were staying with Rex and Ruth, a daughter of William Burton, and what a time we had! Rex and Ruth were members of Scorrier Methodist Church and from Thursday to Sunday night, I preached at Quenchwell. The building was packed every night and visitors came from other Methodist churches. Then on Monday night I delivered a lecture, 'John Wesley – Apostle of England.' There were many questions and discussions and Jeanne and I revelled in the meetings. We had a lovely time with Ruth and Rex and we spent many hours chatting with Mr. Burton.

Again on August 8, 1990, Jeanne and I were back in Cornwall and planning for the Quenchwell Methodist Convention and we spent Thursday 9 to Sunday evening preaching on Romans. The crowds gathered and we had a church full of visitors and we finished up preaching on the Doxology in Romans 16:25 and 26. Everybody seemed glad with the meetings and said that they had not seen in Romans the truth brought out from Thursday to Sunday evening. Jeanne and I stayed with Rex and Ruth and we went places in the afternoons. We were back in Cornwall on Wednesday, August 14, 1991 and we had the church full for every service. On Sunday morning we were invited to preach at Peter Street Methodist Church in St. Ives and we really enjoyed the singing. Peter Street made us welcome and promised to be at Gwennap Pit later that day at 2:30pm.

For a while I had known the Revd. and Mrs. Tom Shaw and he had invited me to preach. We couldn't wait until it was 2:20pm! Gwennap Pit is the largest open air in Cornwall and John Wesley had preached there many times. John and Charles discovered the Pit and Charles wrote: 'I rode back to my own church, the valley near our room at

Gwennap, and found at least five thousand sinners waiting for the glad tidings of salvation.' John Wesley's published accounts of his visits to Gwennap Pit, placed together, form an outline history of the site between 1762 and 1789. Altogether he paid eighteen visits over these years. He was aged fifty-nine when he first used the Pit and eighty-six at his last visit. From the beginning he described the Pit as an amphitheatre.

Sun. Sept. 5, 1762. The wind was so high at five that I could not stand in the usual place at Gwennap. But at a small distance was a hollow, capable of containing many thousands of people. I stood on one side of this amphitheatre toward the top, with people beneath and on all sides, and enlarged on those words from the Gospel for the day. 'Blessed are the eyes which see the things that ye see …. and hear the things which ye hear' (Luke 10:23, 24).

Sun. Sept. 8, 1765. A still larger congregation than the one at Redruth was at Gwennap in the evening, equal to anything I have seen in Moorfields. Yet I think they all heard, while I enforced, 'Why will ye die, O house of Israel?' (Ezekial 18:31 and 33).

Sun. Sept. 11, 1766. The congregation in Redruth was small compared with that which assembled at five in the natural amphitheatre at Gwennap, far the finest I know in the kingdom. It is a round, green hollow, gently shelving down, about fifty feet deep; but I suppose it is two hundred across one way, and near three hundred the other. I believe there were full twenty thousand people; and, the evening being calm, all could hear.

On Sunday, August 23, 1789, he was at Gwennap Pit where he preached his last sermon there, on the healing of Naaman (2 Kings 5:14). He wrote in his *Journal:*

Sun. Aug. 23, 1789. I preached … in the evening at the amphitheatre, I suppose, for the last time; for my voice cannot now command the still increasing multitude. It was supposed that were now more than five-and-twenty thousand. I think it scarce possible that all should hear.

During his eighteen visits Wesley called this place an amphitheatre and no place like that was found in any other place. He spoke to twenty-five thousand men, women and children and that could not be equalled in any others parts of Britain and Ireland. No wonder it is still a place a place of worship two hundred and fifty six years later! Nowadays it's about twelve steps from the bottom to the top and usually in August people attend it regularly. When we arrived we found Bill and ? with their family, all the way from Brooklands. As we were going round the people before it started, we came across Dr. Bowling and Jill, recently appointed as President of the Olivet Nazarene University in Illinois, USA. We had written to him wishing God's blessing and saying that we were going to Cornwall and preaching at Gwennap Pit. Mr. Shaw had told me I could lead and preach and what a mass of people! They sang with all their hearts and it wasn't lost on me to think how many preachers had occupied that spot from Wesley's days. I preached on the *Foolish Farmer* from Luke 12:16-21, and pressed home v.20 and 21. 'But God said to him, "You fool, this night your soul will be required of you: then whose will those things be which you have provided? " So is he who lays up treasures for himself, and is not rich toward God.' It was a wonderful service and I talked with many people afterwards.

John and Jill were invited back to the home of Rex and Ruth and what a time we had there! Rex enquired of John what services they had and the number of full-time evangelists and Rex was shocked to hear that within Illinois there were about four hundred churches. The time was short and after prayer, John and Jill left and we prepared for the evening service. I preached on Acts 26:18 in the Scorrier Methodist Church and there were some seekers. We went home with Rex and Ruth and we stayed up late remembering three great services; at Peter Street Methodist Church, attending and leading the congregation at Gwennap Pit and then the services in Scorrier Methodist Church. Long after we had gone to bed Jeanne and I were saying that God had this planned that we should minister at the Pit.

Altogether I have made fifteen visits to America and on three of these Jeanne went with me. Japan also invited me to preach and on the first visit the Revd. Hiroo Kudo and Mrs. Kudo welcomed me and I stayed in their home. It was the time for Conventions and I had never preached in any language except English. All the preaching was done in their language and I had to preach in English and it was translated into Japanese. I prayed much about this and from the very start, English was the language I preached, with Japanese translations, in sessions of over forty minutes. There were seven hundred in the service and at all the services men and women and young people sought the Lord. Jeanne travelled with me three times to Japan and with all our visits there, the blessing stayed with us. Hiroo was a student at our MA course and it was a delight to welcome Mrs. Kudo and daughter to our college for the degree. Jeanne loved Japan and its people and many times since she has spoken of it and fell in love with its people.

Jeanne and I travelled to Europe three times and visited the people. She was always interested in people and shared their views and testified to her own saving and sanctification. She was in her element when visiting and coming home she reminisced about the people and their living. Gone was the fear of planes and she couldn't wait until the next time. She visited America, Japan, Singapore and Germany and couldn't wait until the next trip.

At this time we were in Leeds and I was down in London preaching at the Thomas Memorial Church of the Nazarene and the Revd. Frank Morley was its pastor. The manse was about a mile and on the Sunday I walked to and from the church. On my way home I stopped to look at the window of an antiques shop and facing me was John Wesley! The shop was closed and I studied it for a long time. It was about six or seven inches high and its profile was clear and intelligent. I pondered it and Frank told me that he would go in when the shop was open and buy it. A week later it arrived and that was my first piece of Wesleyana! So I started to gather pieces and in about twenty years I had three hundred pieces. They were spread around my study and many students and people came to see and admire. I was teaching Wesley Studies and my class came many times to see the growing collection. It all dated back to Mrs. Irvine and the books she had given me; *Forty-Four Sermons*, and, *A Plain Account of Christian Perfection* – and I still have them on my shelves! Slowly but surely it grew and by the time I stepped down from being Principal, the lot had grown to four hundred and twenty pieces. Every place that Jeanne and I visited I looked for Wesley pieces and it soon came about that antiques dealers were contacting me about John and Charles Wesley pieces, and John Fletcher, Adam Clarke, Hugh Bourne, William Clowes, etc. etc. I suppose that I was an expert on the Wesleys, etc. but I never dreamed of that.

Dr. John and Jill Bowling were over at the college and wanted to see the collection. I was explaining to them that I couldn't keep them any longer and John asked me how much they were. We spent a long time discussing these pieces and finally John and Jill offered me a price for three hundred pieces. I accepted and the deal was finished. The price he gave me was enough to buy 7, Albemarle Avenue and I sent the pieces off to the United States to be taken to the Nazarene University in Kankakee, Illinois. This left me with a hundred and twenty pieces and they are round me now in my study. It is forty-four years since I bought my first Wesley piece and I've lost count of how many of them I've talked about and they are still interesting pieces.

In September 1983 I was given the phone number of someone from Staffordshire. I phoned the number but the man replied that he was a Methodist minister but he didn't have any Wesley pieces. He told me of a friend, Dr. Bill Parkes, who had Wesley pieces. I phoned Dr. Parkes who asked me to come down. I met Bill and his wife and within an hour we were best friends. He showed me Wesley pieces and we talked quite a bit about that. Then we broadened the subject and the talk went from each other's experience to suggestion about Wesley meetings. I promised to alert Nazarene ministers and their people and Bill said he would do likewise. Bill booked a room in a nearby Methodist Church and we gathered, about thirty in all. We discussed tactics and the plan was that we would meet twice a year and read some Papers. I was chosen Chairman and Dr. Bill Parkes, Vice-Chairman. Later we were joined by Mr. and Mrs. Paul Taylor, Secretary, Mr. and Mrs. Bill Graham, Editor, and by Revd. and Mrs. Tony Tamburello. We met in September in the Methodist Church and Dr. Skevington

Wood was chosen to read a Paper. The Doctor thrilled us with his Paper on, *Love Excluding Sin*, and when we began to publicize, Dr. Skevington Wood was always saleable.

For thirty years, Jeanne and I attended and Jeanne always played the piano. Eleven o'clock was starting time and we opened with two hymns and then a prayer. As this is a joint production, there are three names we would like to mention.

The Revd. Dr. William Parkes (1933-2001):

I met him quite early in 1984 and had it not been for a phone call that got mixed up, we might never have had the Wesley Fellowship! From 1984 I had worked with him right up to his death in July 2001. He threw himself into working for the Wesley Fellowship and for fifteen years he replied to queries and answered letters. Above all his other gifts he was a preacher of the highest order. I invited him as a guest preacher for our Graduation Service for the Nazarene Theological College, Manchester, 1989, and he 'took off' and preached as only he could. For forty minutes he thrilled the congregation of lecturers and students as exposition, illustration and application poured from him like a torrent. Afterwards a man remarked to me: 'We didn't know there were many who preached like that.' Well, Bill was one of those and in the pulpit he was on fire.

I asked Bill to preach at one of the services at one of the Chapel's weekly services and he held faculty and students as he preached the unsearchable riches of Christ. I invited Bill to preach at one of the services of the Southport Convention. I sat with Jeanne in the congregation and waited for the sermon. He rose up and was immediately into his subject. For fifty minutes he held the people spellbound and it was afterwards that I heard glowing comments and appreciation. Knowing that Bill and I knew each other, a man came to me full of appreciation. 'This was priceless and one of the best preachers I have heard in the Convention or anywhere.' That brother attended each of the services in the Convention and he rated Dr. Bill Parkes so highly.

In all our friendship across these fifteen years, Bill never pushed his ideas, yet all of us admired his careful and exact scholarship, his prodigious knowledge of the vicissitudes of 19th Century Methodism, and the careful scholarship that marked all his written and spoken work. But with all his gifts as preacher, scholarship and writing, he was first and foremost our friend. I was present at Biddulph for the memorial service as Margaret wanted me to preach. In all these fifteen years, I never knew he was a Mayor until I heard someone else say this. In all our conversations, I did not know that he held this office. Plenty of things poured from his lips but he never once mentioned being Mayor!

The Revd. Arthur Skevington Wood (1916-1993):

I met Skevington Wood some time before but on joining the Wesley Fellowship, I came to know him much better. It was a great joy to have him come and deliver our first Lecture, and until he died, he was often at our Fellowship meeting. Bill and I thought he was the man to elect as Honorary President and he distinguished himself in that office. He published thirty books and he was awarded the degree of Doctor of Philosophy and he published his first book in 1957, *Thomas Haweis*, and he went on writing until his death. He produced, *And With Fire* (1958), and his lifelong interest in the Reformation resulted in 1969 with his fine study, *Captive to the Word.* In 1991 came the Maynard James Memorial Lecture, *Third Wave or Second Coming*. His ability as a biblical theologian was illustrated with his, *Paul's Pentecost* (1963), and, *I Want to Know what the Bible Says about God* (1980). As a preacher he dealt with the message, method and motive with his, *Heralds of the Gospel* (1963), and twenty of his sermons were published in 1979, *For All Seasons. William Grimshaw* was published in 1963, and the volume, *The Inextinguishable Blaze* (1960) and, *Brothers in Arms* (1992), were fruits of his Church History and Theology. His finest book was, *The Burning Heart,* written in 1967, not only as a brilliant study of John Wesley as an evangelist but it ranks the best half-dozen ever written on Wesley. That volume achieved something of a record, being in continuous publication from 1967 until 1992. I read it when it was first published and I took it to the College in 1976 and I made it the number one book for a study of John Wesley from 1976 right up to 2009.

In January 1993 Allan Longworth and I went over to visit him in Sheffield and I don't know whether or not Skevington took in it. We spent an hour with him and we talked, prayed and sang one of Charles Wesley's hymns. We returned home and I heard he had died at twelve midnight. The Wesley Fellowship had lost its first President and we were the poorer for his translation. Before his death in 1993, he was doing some work on William Bramwell and the *Preface* to my book, *A Burning and a Shining Light,* has this testimony.

> This present research is a tribute to William Bramwell and to Arthur Skevington Wood; both Wesleyan Christians and both fully committed to preaching the gospel, to soul-saving evangelism and to the hope of heaven-sent revival in the Church. It is my prayer that this brief study of William Bramwell's ministry will be to the glory of God and contribute in some degree to what John Wesley envisioned – a reforming of the Church and the nation and the spreading of 'scriptural holiness over the land.'

There is, however, another reason why I should hold Skevington Wood in the highest esteem. He knew that I was working on my PhD degree and he thought a lot of the subject, *Sufficient Saving Grace: John Wesley's Evangelical Arminianism.* Almost the last thing he did was to borrow my thesis and spend some weeks on it. He called me over to his house in Sheffield and I spent an afternoon going through it with him. He pointed out some markings and asked me to have another look at the material. He was very kind and gentle and he advised me to do my homework thoroughly. It passed without any revision!

The Revd. Dr. Sydney Martin (1910-2004):

Mr. Martin was greatly interested in the work and witness of the Wesley Fellowship. He spent the first five years in the Twecher Church of the Nazarene, Glasgow, and he completed his twenty-five years in the Parkhead Church of the Nazarene. When the Fellowship was first begun in 1984, he complained that there wasn't any interest in Wesley or studies about him. I first met him at the Bundoran Convention,

Donegal, in the south of Ireland in 1957. He was the first preacher that I heard from the Church of the Nazarene and I remember his illustration these sixty-four years! Before the year was out, I was sitting listening to his lectures in Hurlet Nazarene College where I was a student and he gave me an all-absorbing passion for Church History. All the years I was in the ministry he was a good friend and when Bill and I started the Wesley Fellowship, he was in at the beginning and he kept up his membership while he was alive. When letters came from him, both our names were on it. Jeanne marvelled at his message and many a time she was with me when I heard him. He always sent money and said it was doing the work he wanted to be in.

I have been interested in acquiring as many volumes as I could from Dr. John Henry Jowett's books over the years and eventually it numbered twenty-five volumes. Then I heard that Dr. Martin was also keen on Dr. Jowett's volumes and as often as we met we would share our love of Jowett's volumes. In 1970 Dr. Martin managed to acquire the very rare volume of Dr. Jowett's sermons entitled, *Heavens Hallelujah*. This book contains thirty-two sermons preached by Dr. Jowett at Westminster Chapel, London, between 1918 and 1922. Each sermon was issued as a pamphlet and later the collection was bound in an unlettered hard cover and published. It is now a very scarce item and it represents the crown of Dr. Jowett's preaching in the last four years of his ministry. When Dr. Martin retired from the full-time pastoral ministry, he very kindly gave me his copy of, *Heaven's Hallelujah*. This book occupied pride of place on my bookshelf – and then I 'lost' it! All my looking at the Nazarene Theological College row of books and all my looking at my own rows of books failed to spot it. Then it turned up – within about three feet of where I sit! Now the book sits proudly on my shelf.

In 1979 I wrote a letter to Bill McClintock and said that Dr. Martin would love to come to Killadeas Convention. Jeanne was very excited about the invitation and what a week that was! My father and mother went each evening and what a blessing that was. I introduced Dr. Martin and he preached with all his might. One afternoon I invited him to lunch and what a gathering that was. My father and mother loved his preaching and Jeanne and I loved to hear him talk. I reminded them of the Bundoran Convention in 1957 and said that Dr. Martin was the first preacher I had met and how he had blessed me.

In 1989 I wrote a letter to Dr. Martin and said a lecture from him to the Wesley Fellowship would be a delight. We booked 1990 and said he that he was preparing to give a lecture on Wesley's doctrine of assurance. He finished it but he was not well enough to travel. I read it for him but I did wish he could have come down and met the people. There are thirty-one pages to his description and one hundred and thirty-three references. The last reference is worth quoting.

> Finally, in paying tribute to Wesley's unique contribution to the doctrines and experience of the witness of the Spirit, one could not do better than repeat words written by Dr. Yates in his own conclusion. In these he describes Wesley as 'perhaps the master exponent of "experiential" theology – but never at the expense of doctrine, for he was a biblical theologian.' It is but right that we should end on this note for, as we have seen, upon the Bible Wesley took his stand and from this foundation he would not be moved. Our spiritual sire may not have moved the world but he did move a vast number of its inhabitants. He will continue so to do just as long as those who profess to be his kin share his passion – and his foundation.

In 2002 I was invited to Dr. Martin's home with his wife. I took the train to Glasgow and by bus I reached the Martin's house. What a welcome I was given! All of the afternoon we sat and discussed and Dr. Jowett's books especially. The time came for a return to Manchester and we prayed together and I left. I did not see Dr. Martin or Mrs. Martin alive again and all the way to Manchester I went over and over discussion we had had. When he died on August 2, 2004, I travelled up to Glasgow and Parkhead Church of the Nazarene was filled with people who had gathered to wish the family well. The Revd. Colin Wood, ThB, MA, LTRC, gave a fine and moving address and Dr. Hugh Rae gave a moving tribute. He talked about his first meeting with Dr. Martin and his friendship with him down the years. Afterwards we attended Mearns Cemetery, South Glasgow burial ground, where we laid his body to rest, waiting for the resurrection of the just. All the way home to Manchester I kept thinking of the years I had known Dr. Martin and the fine sermons he had delivered.

In 1964 Jeanne, Stephen and I went over to Whitehill North, Irvinestown, and what a welcome awaited us. My father and mother welcome us and we knew now that we were home. Jeanne had never been to Ireland and all of it was strange. We made our way to the Killadeas Convention and heard Revd. Duncan Campbell and Major Alistair Smith. We had no transport and we relied on others to take us. In 1967 we made the same crossing but now we had a minibus and Stephen and Jonathan were with us. We visited Killadeas Convention and heard the Revd. Ieuan Jones and the Revd. Leonard Ravenhill. What a wonderful platform speaker was Leonard Ravenhill and he preached every night. Jeanne loved to hear him and the week passed too quickly. We were back again in 1971 and new preachers joined in the services; Revd. Sam Ennis and Revd. Herbert McGonigle. Sam Ennis led the singing and for the first time I preached. What a wonderful service and men and women who had known me in the past told me of their blessing. From 1971 until the finish of the Killadeas Convention in 2006, Jeanne and I attended twenty-nine such gatherings and out of them I am going to pick certain preachers who were a blessing to Jeanne and myself.

The Revd. Duncan Campbell:

Mr. Campbell came to Killadeas eight times, beginning in 1960 and finishing in 1969. From the start his ministry was on the Cross and the dynamic power of the Holy Spirit. He had been used by God in the awakening in Lewis and his sermons were peppered with stories and experiences. From the start Mr. Campbell was rooted in the Bible and he spoke with a Highland accent and each sermon was an hour long. Nobody smiled during the service and it was illustrations and deeply held convictions that held the people for an hour. At the close a hymn was sung and closing prayer and then people hung about trying to find an opportunity to talk to Mr. Campbell. All that week people were wondering if God was going to pour out His Spirit on the people. When in the morning a prayer meeting was held that lasted two hours, there were mighty prayers for revival and as Mr. Campbell spoke in eight of the Campmeetings Revival, there were pleas for revival coming from hundreds of people. Jeanne and I were listening to Mr. Campbell and a deep longing for revival was born in our hearts.

Dr. Dale Yocum:

Dr. Yocum came to the Camp three times in 1970, 1971 and 1980, and Jeanne and I were there in all three meetings. From the start Dr. Yocum was a holiness preacher and we got on well. He was from Kansas City and he knew that it was the Church of the Nazarene and he knew a lot of people from the Churches' headquarters. Night after night he was preaching and as we listened to his sermons it was a great experience. On the Sunday he asked to preach at the morning service in Enniskillen Independent Methodist Church and he took as his text the words of Exodus 32:6; 'The people sat down to eat and drink, and rose up to play.' It was a mighty message and the people were talking about it long after. Dr. Yocum was there the next year and we enjoyed him first and last. We were there again in 1980 and the news came through that he was ill at the airport and he had to be rushed back to Kansas City and in a month he was dead. He was a top preacher and he held Killadeas Convention in awe.

The Revd. Tom Shaw:

Mr. Shaw was at Killadeas Convention seven times and he never failed to deliver a sermon that challenged the people. He pastored the Congregational Church in Ballycraigy, Co. Antrim, and on one occasion he was asked to sing William Cowper's hymn, 'There is a fountain filled with blood.' He was asked to sing again in the services and each time he thrilled us. He was Chairman of the Faith Mission and I knew him because he had invited me to preach at Ballycraigy Convention. Tom Shaw was meant to be a preacher and each time he visited the Killadeas Convention, he was in his element. Jeanne and I watched him in the Convention and we were never disappointed and whenever he spoke he was very well received. Jeanne took pen and paper and when we got home the notes were discussed.

The Revd. John Harris:

John and Gretta came to the Killadeas Campmeeting and right from the start he was a popular preacher. Gretta was the daughter of Mr. and Mrs. Loane of Manoo. John and Gretta were members of the Elim Church and he was the Pastor and when he came to us, he branched out and was taking meetings all over the place. John was a very devoted student of the Bible and he revelled in it. John and I became good friends and we shared the pulpit in almost every meeting, including the final one. In the final meeting (though we did not know of the events), the Killadeas Convention was packed that Sunday as John and I prepared for the final services. John preached at 3pm and the hall was full. The evening service was timed for 8pm but the people started arriving just before seven. The meeting was packed and many stood around, being unable to find a seat. I preached on Luke 17:32. 'Remember Lot's wife.' At the close we all stood up and, as usual, the hymn was sung, 'When the trumpet of the Lord shall sound.' What a service! What a gathering! What singing! As John and I stood at the door, no one realised that was the last service.

In 2002 I published a book, *To God Be The Glory,* and it marked he fiftieth year since Killadeas had begun. The Foreword was written by Mr. Bill McClintock and gives thanks to God for pouring out His Spirit upon the meetings from 1952 until 2002. He writes: 'The emphasis was on prayer, brokenness before God, revival and holiness of life.... The purpose of this booklet is to thank God for raising up this Convention and blessing it all down the years for half a century.' St. Paul spoke of his ministry in terms of declaring 'the whole counsel of God' (Acts 20:27), and the same could be said on the Convention. Its four glorious truths are these: **The Gospel of the New Birth, The Gospel of Assurance, The Gospel of the Spirit-Filled Life**, and, **The Gospel of Christ's Second Coming**. All the preachers are listed from 1952 until 2002 and it has fifteen photographs and testimonies of fifteen people.

Jeanne and I were privileged to attend thirty-eight of these great meetings and we will always be blessed by its services.

On the January 7, 2007, Mr. McClintock passed away and there was deep appreciation for the years he had spent in Co. Fermanagh. He was born on July 3, 1912 at Cooneen, near Fivemiletown. Following local schooling he went to on to Greenmount Agricultural College, then to Queens' University. Following graduation he came to Enniskillen in 1935 to take up the post of County Agricultural Organiser (later Officer). He soon developed a good rapport with the local farming community and over the next forty-two years he was known as 'the farmers' friend.' In 1939 he married Gladys Grant and three daughters were born to them; Margaret, Pauline and Sandra.

Converted to Christ as a teenager aged 17 as a result of attending an open-air service, the young Bill McClintock, as he was known to so many, devoted himself to Christian service. By the time he arrived in Enniskillen in 1935 he was already conducting services and missions in many places, a ministry that continued until about four weeks before his death. In 1947 he invited the Revd. W. P. Nicholson, Ulster's greatest-ever evangelist, to hold evangelistic services in the Presbyterian Church in Enniskillen. This was Mr. Nicholson's only mission in Co. Fermanagh and there were lasting conversions. In 1952 he organised Fermanagh's first-ever 'Campmeeting' Conventions which became the annual Killadeas Convention. Although he retired in 1977 from his agricultural office, there was no retirement from the work of God. On both sides of the border he travelled to preach in churches and mission halls, taking part in open-air services and engage in door-to-door visitation and tract distribution to residents and visitors in Enniskillen. He was best known for his Saturday morning open-air meetings at the Diamond. With some supporting friends he conducted these services for sixty-six years. He also devoted many hours every week to hospital visitation and the homes of elderly friends.

I crossed over to Belfast on Thursday, January 11, and there I was met by Denzil and Marina McIlfatrick and we proceeded down to

Colebrook Parish Church which was packed for his funeral service. Two of his favourite hymns were sung; 'What a friend we have in Jesus,' and, 'To God be the glory.' In his funeral tribute I used the words of King David in 2 Samuel 3 to describe him. 'Today a great man and a prince is fallen in Israel.' For well over sixty years William T. McClintock was wonderfully used of God in Co. Fermanagh and further afield to influence people for Christ, for the gospel and the cause of Christian missions at home and abroad. What John Bunyan said of Mr. Valiant-for-Truth in his, *Pilgrim's Progress*, can be said of Brother McClintock's Home-call. 'He crossed the river and the angels sounded their trumpets on the other side.'

There were some of us who wondered what would be the outcome of the Killadeas Convention. This was worrying to Gladys McClintock and she wrote me a letter saying that it had run its course and it would be wise to close it down. I answered her and said that I would call a meeting and see if all the others felt the same. I arrived in Belfast to be picked up by Denzil McIlfatrick and went to the church. Mr. Tom McDaniels, Revd. John Harris, Mr. Bertie Johnson, Mr. Hyland Mitchell and roughly fifteen of us turned up. It had been running fifty-five years and the fruits of it had gone to the ends of the earth. For four hours we discussed it plainly and we came to the conclusion that it would be wise to close it down. There were quite a few tears at its closure but eventually it had to cease. We stood and sang the hymn that always closed the Killadeas Convention, 'When the trumpet of the Lord shall sound, and time shall be no more.' I closed the meeting in prayer and we all said our goodbyes.

My mother lived alone in the house for four years and by that time she was tired and moved to my sister Mary's for rest. She finally went to Joe and Ethel and finished her ninety third year. I was in Cullybackey Methodist Church taking services where the Revd Dr. Turner, was minister. One day John said to me that he would run me down to Golan, Trillick, Co. Tyrone, to see my mother. She was delighted to see us and we spent two hours with her. When it was time to go, John read the scriptures and prayed. Then I kissed her and we left. Two months later we heard the news that she was gone. I attended the funeral and the Revd. William Parks, minster of the Independent Methodist Church, Enniskillin, gave a wonderful word of the gospel and told how my mother was saved in 1955 and gave herself to the Lord. She was laid in the graveyard beside her husband waiting for the resurrection of that glorious morning. I paused and wonder where I would have been if my mother had not been saved. She faithfully prayed for me, morning and evening, from 1955, until her death in 1993.

After we had moved to Manchester, we started going to Salford Church of the Nazarene and we very happy with the church. The Revd. Geoff Austin was pastor and he was soon very interested in Stephen and Jonathan. After some years he left and while waiting for a pastor, I was chosen to fill the spot – and it lasted five years! Jeanne was pianist and we loved the church. There were about forty people and some twenty-five turned up for the Monday night prayer meeting. Prayer was important and every Monday saw the people turning up. The atmosphere was terrific and we saw God answering prayer.

I remember the year 1992 and we were at Killadeas Convention and we wondered at the time whether we would be back for Jonathan's first child, Joseph. We hurried to Manchester and there were scenes of great joy as Jeanne and I held Joseph! Jeanne was beside herself with joy – Joseph was our first grandchild!! She loved him with all her heart and there were many times we had Joseph to ourselves. Four years later, while we were holidaying in Ireland, we learned that another baby had arrived – a girl called Lucy! Jeanne was filled with praise for giving us a granddaughter for she herself had borne three sons! Our grandchildren were loved by us and all through childhood they were welcome in our home. On Sunday morning we used to take them to church and they loved being with us. One day Jeanne had asked where the names came from and Jonathan admitted that my parents were called Joe and Lucy! Jeanne was thrilled with the news and admitted that Joe and Lucy were familiar!

We left the church in 2011 and transferred to Manchester Brooklands. Most of the people we knew and we soon settled into worship. Revd. Karl Standfield ThB, MA, was minister. Karl came to College in 1981 and I was his lecturer in Church History, Wesley Studies and Homiletics. We enjoyed the church and its people and Jeanne accompanied me until she stopped coming in September 2016.

Jeanne and I were brought into contact with Mr. and Mrs. Fred and Wendy and we were invited there on Sunday, February 7, 1993. We met them and something started on the personal level that has lasted all these years. Fred and Wendy were in charge of Altofts Hebron Church and through all the years we have always stayed in their home and it has always been a blessing to Jeanne and myself. We got to know Randy and Gaynor and the six of us have always made it special for all our visits. Looking at my diary we have been there seventy-eight times! Starting there in 1993 we have been there both Saturday and Sunday and Saturday was given over to lectures on the Church. Right from the start we always met around the Lord's Table and what precious times they were. Fred and Randy always ministered at the table and the rest of the time was given over to hearing the word of God. What singing! What a joy! What a fellowship! Jeanne and I loved it there and always we went with open hearts. Fred, Wendy, Randy and Gaynor made it over to Manchester and what times of blessing we had with them. I kept every text that I preached upon and my first sermon in 1993 was from Revelation 2:1-7, 'Losing the First Love.' My final sermon was on Matt. 16:13-20; 'Who Is Jesus Christ?'

Jeanne and I met the family of John and Mrs. Herons on Saturday, June 13, 1992, when we were asked to go to South Shields Church. Jeanne was enthusiastic about going for she went there at about eleven years of age. Jeanne's father was appointed a civil servant and she was excited about seeing the place. John and Pat were living in Cleadon, South Shields and their two boys. Right away we were friends and that has lasted ever since. Ten times I preached in the People Mission and every time Jeanne was with me. We enjoyed fellowship with John and Pat and the rest of their family.

The Revd. Harold and Dorothy Moore were active in South Chadderton Methodist Church in Oldham, and we met them on the November 16, 1986, as they attended the gathering of the Wesley Fellowship at the Nazarene Theological College, and Harold read a paper on Charles Wesley's hymns. On Sunday, November 16, he invited me to preach at their services and I took as my sermon, 'Teach Us To Pray,' as recorded in Luke 11:1, and in the evening, 'Thirsting For God,' as recorded in Matt. 5:1-12. On Sunday, 30, 1988, he invited us to the services and I took Hebrews 2:1-9 and preached on 'So Great Salvation,' and in the evening on 'David's Epitaph,' in Acts 13:22. When Harold and Dorothy moved to up to Darlington, they invited us eleven times and Jeanne was always able to be with me. We enjoyed Darlington and over all these years, we enjoyed both the services and staying with Harold and Dorothy. They are a loving couple and since Jeanne has gone to be with our Lord, the telephone is a handy service. Harold has sent me his writing books and I have done the same.

Now it is time to speak of the times we have spent in Ireland when Dad and Mum were laid to rest. On a Monday morning after the Campmeeting was over, Jeanne and I decided to travel around the north of Ireland, starting off at Donegal. We stayed several hours in Donegal and then set out for Milltown and Killybegs. We loved the mountains and the waters of Donegal Bay and we stayed the night in Killybegs. In the morning we headed for Glencolumbkille and we followed the road that leads to Common Bridge and then about four miles to Ardara. It was lovely and we enjoyed seeing Loughros More Bay and the surrounding islands. After that we followed the R261 to Dunglow. The country was beautiful and we wandered round the town looking at its buildings. We headed north on the N56 and came to Dunfanaghy and then we headed south on the N56 and came to Letterkenny. The next morning we were on the road N14 and within four miles we crossed the border and found ourselves in Londonderry. We crossed onto the A2 road and came to Limavady and then the A2 road that leads to Coleraine. We stayed the night in Coleraine and then headed on for Portstewart and Porthrush. The scenery was lovely and we enjoyed motoring along the coast, including Portballintrae, Balltoy and Ballycastle.

We left Ballycastle in the morning and motored down, still on the A2, as far as Cushendall, Waterfoot, Glanarm, Ballygally, and then on to Larne. We left Larne in the morning and again travelling on the A2, came to Whiteside, Carrickfergus, Newtownabbey, Belfast and then headed for Holywood, Bangor, Donaghadee, Ballywalter, Ballyhalbert, Portavogie, and then on to Portaferry. We sat a long time at Portaferry and watched the boats crossing to Stranford. The week was up and every night we thanked God for permitting us to see a beautiful part of the Republic of Ireland and the North.

In 1996 we were again at the Killadeas Convention and we heard that a Mr. and Mrs. Swanson, who lived at Skibbereen, Co. Cork, had a meeting once a week and they were wondering if Jeanne and I would take the meeting, held at their house every Friday evening. We arranged to take the meeting and Jeanne and I left Enniskillen and turned west and we arrived at Belcoo, and then onto the N16, arriving at Manorhamilton and then on to Sligo. We left Sligo on the N4 and arrived at Collooney, and then on to N17, arriving at Tobercurry and then Charlestown. We spent the night in Charlestown, and then took the N17 to Claremorris, and then down to Tuam. Travelling right on the N17 we reached Galway Bay. It was beautiful and we followed the R336 on to Tully, right along the road, bounded on the left by Galway Bay. It was wonderful and Jeanne and I stopped for a while at Furbo and at Loughaunbeg. We stayed the night in Tully and next morning we retraced our steps and on to the N6, taking us to Gort and we arrived at Limerick. We took the N20 that led us to Arare, Rathkeale, Newcastle West, Abbeyfeale, Castleislaneland and Killarney. We settled there in a B&B, and then set out on the N71, through Kenmare, Bantry and then on to Skibbereen. We followed the map to the Swanson's house and we were given a hearty welcome. Their friends started to arrive and it was 9pm before it started. There was a room holding forty people and it was full. They asked me to lead the service and preach and the Lord heard us and we rejoiced at the service and the blessing received. Then it was tea and they did not go home until it was past midnight! Mr. and Mrs. Swanson kept us talking and it was three o'clock before we finally got to sleep.

The next morning we had breakfast, then a prayer together and we were off. All day we talked about the Swansons and it was lovely to meet them. Skibbereen is the furthest town in Ireland and it is six miles from the sea. We headed for the N17 and passed through Clonakilty, Bandon and Cork, and then the N8 which took us through Fermoy, Mitchelstown, Cahir, Cashel, and we turned left onto the N62, and that took us to Thurles, Templemore, Roscrea, Birr, and Athlone. We stopped and had dinner, looked round the town and then set out. We motored up the N55 to Edgeworthstown, and then took up the N4 as far as Carrich-on-Shannon. We left on the R209 and passed Drumshanbo and took the R207 which landed us on the A4 at Belcoo, Letterbreen and on to Enniskillen. Jeanne and I thanked the Lord for journeying with us and we finally arrived at Ballinamallard, Co, Fermanagh, where we stayed with Tom and Anna. We had covered two hundred and fifty miles since we left Skibbereen, and all the way home it was hot and sunny. Tom and Anna wanted to know all the places we had covered and it was past midnight before we broke up and went to bed.

In view of the College opening in September, Jeanne and I had a little time to spend and it was the last week in August when we set out to visit the north east coast. The year was 1997 and we set off in the morning of August 25, and Jeanne was thrilled that she didn't have to cook any food for a week. We made the journey by car, and, setting off at 9am, we journeyed on the M62 as far as the M1 north, up past Garforth, and on until we reached the A1M, going north. We travelled up the motorway past Wetherby, and on up to Disforth, then on the A1, past Scotch Corner, and found the A1M and the A690 into Sunderland. We hadn't realised that it was the schools holiday and every B&B we tried was full. Eventually we found one on the coast at Seaton and there we stayed the night. We were up early and the dining room was two floors up and we were the only guests. We went in and the breakfast was laid out for two and the seats were in the window. What a view! Looking out through the window we could see the Atlantic Ocean just one hundred yards away. We sat on with the lady and she told us that this room was special because there was a view that no-one could beat. We talked with the lady for a while and, eventually we had to go. Going outside we saw the Atlantic Ocean and for miles and miles we kept it in view. We proceeded north on the coast and stopped often to admire the view. We motored on until we reached Whitburn and spent the morning down on the beach. Then we proceeded on the A183 until we saw Marsden Bay and we stopped there a good while.

The next stop was South Shields, and Jeanne was in her element! Forty years back she remembered her sister Pam and her parents coming here from London and her father was offered a job in the civil service. We drove round and there was the house that she and her parents had lived in! She remembered well and told me that in those days she worshipped at the Nazarene Church! - not the official Church of the Nazarene. We stayed there a long time and eventually we had to leave. The next town was Tynemouth and, four miles distant was Whitely Bay. We found a B&B and we stayed there until morning. Jeanne was surprised to find all that she knew was gone and she told me that South Shields was one of her favourite spots.

In the morning we motored on and we came to Seaton Sluice and on to Blyth. The weather was lovely and we left the A193 and joined the B1334 to Newbiggin-by-the-Sea. We stayed there a while, looking round the shops and wandering by the sea shore. We headed inland a few miles and then took up the A189, followed it and joined the A1068 and followed it up to join the A1 still going north. We travelled on up the A1 until we saw the sign that said Holy Island. We stopped and stayed a long time looking at Holy Island and the burial of so many people in that spot, said to be watched over by the prayers of so many thousands. Neither Jeanne nor I had been there before and there was something that held us wondering what it was that kept us there for so long. We eventually left that spot and motored on until we reached Berwick-upon-Tweed. We stayed the night in a B&B and next morning we came to Coldstream, over the border into Scotland. We stayed there a long time examining the town, and then we headed on to Kelso, Jedburgh and straight down the A68 crossing into England and we came to Corbridge. We stayed in Hexham overnight and the next morning we journeyed to Haydon Bridge and then we journeyed on down the A686 to Penrith, taking up the M6, and arriving home at 8pm. Our wonderful week was up and we gave God thanks and praise for seeing so many wonderful places.

We arranged to be away for a week and we left home on the Monday, August 26, 2002, and decided to travel to Wales. We had not been to Wales except for Church services and it was Jeanne who decided that week should be spent in Wales. We left the house quite early and we picked up the M56, then the M53 and this took us to Wrexham. We walked around the town and stayed there quite a while and took interest in the houses. We joined the A5 and it took us to Ruabon, and turning right, we picked up the A5 which took us to Llangollen and on to Betws-y-Coed. We stopped there a while and visited the shops. We journeyed to Bethesda and turning right, we followed the A55 and came to Menai Bridge. It was a busy place and we had dinner looking out to see all the cars and lorries and buses waiting to cross into Anglesey. We joined the traffic and what an experience it was to be on the island. We turned right and what an experience it was cars and buses and a straight, open road. We journeyed to Pentraeth, Llanallgo, Burwen, Lladdeusant and Llanynghened, and watched the cars and buses running along to Holyhead and then to Ireland. It was glorious weather and we sat and watched them depart. We joined the A55 back to the Menai Bridge, turned left and settled for the night in a B&B.

The next morning we joined the A487 and came to Caernarfon. We looked around the town and the University and then took our leave and made it as far as Llandwrogand then journeyed on to the A499 right down to Pwllheli. It was crowded with people and we spent a while there on the beach. Afterwards we went to Penthos, Llanbedrog and into Abersoch. Again the sun was shining and the crowds made it a crush finding chairs. Abersoch is the last town on the western side of

Lleyn Peninsula and it is overcrowded. We journeyed back along the A497 to Porthmadog and then took the A487 to Maentwrog and immediately turned right on the A496 to Harlech. We joined the crowds and visited the scenes, then on to Barmouth. The sea was beautiful and we sat a long time gazing out over Barmouth Bay. The road from Harlech to Barmouth runs along the shore and for ten miles the sea was our shore and it was lovely. We spent the night in a B&B and we were up the next morning and heading for Llanellyde.

We turned left on to the A470 and after about three miles, we turned right on the A470 and after four miles on to the A487 to Machylleth and stopped there for lunch. Then we moved on and after twenty miles, Aberystwyth came into view and the site was glorious. We spent many hours in Aberystwyth and then drove along the A487; a glorious road and Cardigan Bay was so magnificent and we stopped at Llanrhystud, Llanon and Abereron. Eventually we reached Cardigan and stopped there for tea. Following the A484 we reached Newcastle Emlyn and stayed there for the night. We had seen beautiful countryside before, in Ireland, Scotland and England but the places we had just seen rivalled them. Going to bed at about midnight, we talked long after about the beauty of the Wales scene. Wales has some of the best scenery we have seen anywhere.

In the year 2003, Jeanne said to me that instead of booking a night here and there for our next week, we should take B&B and stay in it while we were on holiday. We rented a room in Scarborough for a week and drove there and settled down in the room and consulted the map. It was a real joy to be in Yorkshire for we had been there over the years and the weather was fine and sunny and we looked forward to the week. On Sunday morning we worshipped at the Methodist Church, a building that could seat one thousand people but just forty turned up. The service was fine and we enjoyed it, and while we were at coffee after the service, Jeanne managed to drop a word that I was Principal of the Nazarene College in Manchester! Immediately people gathered around me and asked, if they invited me, would we come? I replied that I should consider this and left it there but eventually there was no invitation. After looking around the town, we had lunch and sat and listened to the band playing in the park. We had dinner in the B&B and then walked round the streets. We didn't imagine that the crowds would be out but Scarborough is a town that invites people.

After breakfast we motored through Filey and Bridlington and settled there for the day. We looked around the town and, after lunch, we settled down in our folding chairs and watched the sun bring out the visitors. Every place was booked and we enjoyed the afternoon. We headed back to Scarborough and enjoyed our evening meal. The distance was not too great and we enjoyed all we saw.

The next morning after breakfast we headed north on the A171 and turning right we entered Flyingthorpe and saw Robin Hood's Bay. We took great care in descending the hill and came to the shops. It was told that in Robin Hood's time there was not any outlaw that could match him in any sport and the brave outlaw covered himself with glory by escaping the gallows. It seems another world to us and we looked carefully round and had tea in one of the shops. By following the B1447 we reached High Hawsker and took the road that led into Whitby. The town is lovely and we had been there many times before. We parked in a car park and began to explore the town. It's divided into two by a bridge that is lifted and lowered about every two hours and it's great to see the bridge being lifted. We explored the Abbey and took photographs of it and all the grounds. There were plenty of shops selling John Wesley memorabilia but we didn't buy anything as we had them all! We finished looking at shops and took the road, the A171, that led us back into Scarborough and managed to make it by 7pm and the time that dinner was made. After the meal we discussed Whitby and all it had to lure the crowds and reckoned that it was full every day.

The next day we explored Scarborough and we bought things for the family and a number of presents for ourselves. The day was beautiful and we explored caves and caverns. Eventually we had had enough and returned to our B&B in time for dinner. The next day we headed for Filey and we took chairs and sat for most of the day. We talked

36

much about Scarborough and reckoned that it must be one of the places people visit when in Yorkshire. All the days spent in that lovely spot were wonderful and we didn't see a drop of rain the whole week.

Eventually Friday came and we left for home. After about an hour we came to fields blue with lavender and we stopped and started to look round. We discovered that there are many areas of cooking in Yorkshire in which use lavender. Jeanne loved the spot and we spent three hours looking around. Lavender has for many centuries been used as a flavouring and condiment and has now found its way back into cooking. Very versatile for sweet dishes, infused lavender can be used in milk puddings, ice cream and sorbets. We roamed the fields and wondered if they had known its deep riches. The Yorkshire gift shop contains many products including lavender and we saw candles, oil burners, sticks and sprays, as well as lavender fragrant products. The shop started selling pure lavender and then branched out selling herbs, grasses, alpines and wildflowers, lavender biscuits, lavender honey beer, lavender conserves and much, much more. Inside the shop Jeanne went round and smelt the lavender and wondered at its products. We had tea and lavender biscuits and Jeanne took up the products and discussed them with the staff. Eventually I told Jeanne that we must pursue our journey and with many a backward look, she finally left!

We were very happy in my Principalship and we enjoyed it up until June 2004. The Board of Governors had arranged our farewell on Saturday, June 12, 2004, and we were invited to join the friends gathered in Emmanuel Church, Didsbury, at 7:30pm. Jeanne, Jonathan and his two children, Joe and Lucy, Keith, Revd. Fred Cowan, and I attended and the church was full of people, joining in praising the Lord for the past eighteen years. The service was led by the District Superintendent of the British Isles Northern District, the Revd. Colin H. Wood, and the Revd. Dr. Hugh Rae was asked to bring the sermon. Many tributes were read, including those of Dr. John C. Bowling, President of Olivet Nazarene University, Dr. Jerry D. Lambert, Education Commissioner of the Church of the Nazarene, Dr. Ron

Benefial, President of the Nazarene Theological Seminary, Kansas City, Dr. Franklin Cook, Eurasia Region, Revd. John Haines, Eurasia Regional Education Coordinator, and Dr. Alex R.G. Deasley, Professor Emeritus, Nazarene Theological, Kansas City, USA. Dr. Rae told the congregation that I came from Northern Ireland, in my eighteen years had pastored three churches and had finally made the College in 1976. In 1986 I was appointed Principal and held that office for eighteen years. In that period the College had moved on and now had two hundred and fifty students. The College had obtained the commitment to give the BA programme and Manchester University had arranged to vet the College every five years. The next programme was obtaining the MA degree and further studies into the PhD for those who were successful in applying for its course.

There is one example of the service that I would like to mention. Our son Stephen and his wife, were away on holiday but he wrote a letter that was read out to the people.

Dear Dad,

I'm sorry that Janice and I were unable to be at this evening's event, however I can assure you that you are in our thoughts. So the time has finally arrived for you to step down as the Principal. It seems only a short time ago that we were all in the college for your inauguration as the Principal. You may recall that I and my friend Ian had returned from our first holiday abroad in Greece to be at that event. There is a photograph on the piano at home taken on that day, and both you and I had more hair then!

Your being at the college has always been a source of pride for all the family, not in a vain sense, rather in the sense that we knew you were doing the job that you loved and felt called to, and there are few in this day and age who can say that with certainty. It is fair to say that the college has been a major part of your life, from the pictures I've seen of a slim young man with wavy hair, to the silver incarnation that you are now. I know that you have always felt deeply about the work of preparing for the Ministry and other aspects of Christian service. I know well the many hours of diligent preparation that went into your work, and I know that there are many who have benefited from this and have cause to thank you. I can also say that you have always had time for your family, and that I am grateful for this. Whether it was being a Pastor, lecturer or Principal,

you were never too busy for us and we thank you for that. But the reality is that you are not hanging up your proverbial mortarboard for good, rather I seem to think that you'll be returning to your first love, preaching and teaching. Have a lovely evening.
Steve and Janice.

The Family
Front row: Keith Romig, Jeanne, Herbert, Janice
Back row: Joe, Stephen, Jonathan, Lucy

I stepped down from the Principalship in 2004 and the Revd. Dr. David McCullough, whom Dr. Rae and myself had interviewed, was installed. I moved to the room in the White House and for the next five years, I was taken up lecturing on Church History, Wesley Studies and the MA programme and by 2009 I had nine PhD students. I loved the College and was in every day from Tuesday to Thursday. Jeanne and I had invitations to preach at churches all over Ireland, Scotland and England and we enjoyed all those visits. Fortunately I had a record of every sermon I preached from going to Ashton Church of the Nazarene on Sunday, September 19, 1976, to Hebron Church, Altofts, on Sunday, June 7, 2009.

I was sitting in our garden with Jeanne on Monday, June 8, 2009, reading a book when, without warning, I suffered a stroke. I was rushed into Wythenshaw Hospital and was there three weeks. I don't remember much about it and how glad I was to welcome Jeanne twice a day and see Keith, Stephen, Jonathan, Bill and Lorraine Graham, Fred and Wendy from Altofts, and many others. The time passed slowly and after twenty-three days, I was allowed home with Stephen driving. The first three months I just don't remember but from that time, more and more events keep coming back. Jeanne was with me all the time and with her love and care and comfort, things began slowly but surely to come to me. I was hard on myself and walked two or three times around the block. For those first three or four months, health visitors and nurses kept coming as I slowly recovered.

After six months I was able again to drive the car and we went to church regularly. Jeanne and I had been very much at home in the Salford Church but as things passed, we often went to the Brooklands Church of the Nazarene and we began to feel that it was time to leave. We had been in the Salford Church of the Nazarene thirty four years and we decided to leave. There was only one church for us and we had known Karl and Ingrid so many years and Bill and I were friendly all these years. We went gladly to Brooklands Church and the welcome we received was wonderful. Now that Jeanne has been gone eighteenth months, I miss her every day but I am glad for our church at Brooklands and the friendship is wonderful. It is good to be worshipping with around ninety people and Karl pastors and preaches every Sunday and I often tell him that it was wonderful today!

Jeanne and I attended every year at Graduation in the Whitworth Hall in the University of Manchester and I didn't know what was coming in the 2014 Graduation. Jeanne had been alerted and all of the faculty but the surprise was that I should be included with a book written by scholars in honour of me. The book is, *The Path of Holiness: Perspectives in Wesleyan Thought in Honour of Herbert B. McGonigle,* and the editors are Dr. Joseph W. Cunningham, my student, and the Revd. Dr. David Rainey. Covering 198 pages, this essay has ten contributors; Dr. Ron Benefiel, Dr. Kent Brower, Dr. Kenneth J. Collins, Dr. Joseph W. Cunningham, Dr. Phil Meadows, Dr. Thomas A. Noble, Dr. Henry Rack, Dr. David Rainey, Dr. Ian Randall, Dr. Joseph Wood. I was staggered at the thought and I was just able to thank Dr. David Rainey, currently a Senior Lecturer in Theology and all of those who had contributed to the work. In paying me the honour of a book, Dr. Cunningham and Dr. Rainey had this to say.

> This book serves to honour the life and work of Dr. Herbert B. McGonigle, former principal and lecturer of Nazarene Theological College, Manchester. His lifelong commitment to scholarship and teaching as well as his service for the Church of the Nazarene in Great Britain have made a lasting contribution both to the field of Wesley Studies and to numerous students who have gone on to parish work and other forms of ministry. Recognised internationally for his expertise in Wesley Studies, Dr. McGonigle is a scholar of first rate, a beloved teacher, and an unwavering mentor to the students and colleagues privileged to study and work with him. What unites each specialism underneath the banner 'Wesleyan,' is the centrality of holiness to Wesleyan discourse and this truth is exemplified in Dr. McGonigle's work on the life, thought, and legacy of John Wesley, but most importantly, it is evident in the kind of life he has always led in relation to those privileged to call him colleague and friend.

While I live, this book remains on my shelves!

While I was working at the college for thirty-four years, I had gathered up a collection of John and Charles' work nearing one thousand volumes. I had used these in lectures and teaching but getting over my stroke, teaching was a thing of the past. I donated them to Nazarene Theological College and they put my name on each one. In the days to come, all students, glancing at the title, will have room to give thanks for my efforts. I have kept at home about six hundred books, including, *The Works of John Wesley,* 14 volumes; Nazarene Publishing House, Kansas City, Missouri; *The Works of John Wesley*, Oxford, 19785 and Abingdon Press, Nashville, Vols. 19; *The Letters of John Wesley*, John Telford, 8 Vols. 1931; *The Journal of John Wesley*, 8 vols. 1938, Nehemiah Curnock; *A Christian Library, consisting of Extracts from and abridgements of the Choicest Pieces of Practical Divinity*, 30 volumes, by John Wesley, 1819 -1824; *Wesley's Veterans*, 7 volumes, London, Roberts Culley; *The Poetical Works of John and Charles Wesley*, 13 Vols. G. Osborn, 1868-1872; *The Works of The Rev. John Fletcher*, Vols. 1-9, Joseph Benson, 1859; etc. etc.

In handing over a thousand books, I was called to the college and thanked by its Principal, Dr. Deirdre Brower Latz, for thinking of the college. The Revd. Irvine Grey and Hyland Mitchell were there from Northern Ireland, and lecturers with whom I had served. During that interview I was surprised to see a film, *Emeritus: The Life and Times of Revd. Dr. Herbert McGonigle*, and almost all of the staff. The film began with southern Ireland in 1939 and it lasted about thirty minutes. Dr. Julie Lunn was its commentator and the Revd. Irvine Grey took part, alongside Dr. Peter Rae, Dr. Thomas Noble, the Revd. Colin Wood, Dr. Deirdre Brower Latz, the Revd. Fred Cowan, Dr. Kent Brower, Dr. David Bunday and Bill Graham. I felt emotional as the film pictured Mum and Dad, my marriage to Jeanne in 1961, our boys and the evidence of my thirty-five years and all the people I had met. A copy of the film is now in my hands and its production was made during the spring but, for me, Jeanne didn't see it made. She would be so proud of the film and all of the people Jeanne and I met during those years.

Herbert and Jeanne McGonigle c.1961

There are dear people whom I would love to mention. When I was attending Manoo Mission Hall before I went to college, I first met Tom McDaniels. He came to Manoo quite often and I often spoke with him about his message. He was a dear friend and when I was asked to preach at Killadeas Convention, he offered Jeanne and I accommodation. We met Anna, his wife, and immediately there sprung up a friendship that has never ceased. We used to go to Rossnowlagh, Co. Donegal, on the Monday after the Campmeetings, and the four of us enjoyed the visit. We were looking out on St. John's Point and many a year we spent in talking about Killadeas Convention and talked together about the services. Tom was there at the meeting as we discussed Killadaes Convention and came to the conclusion that it was all over. Tom was a fine Christian man and then the Lord took him Home.

John and Audrey McClellant came to us every year and they have proved to be very loving friends. I have known them over forty-five years and having them in our home was a blessing indeed. Jeanne loved to see them coming and all the time we were together, Jeanne and Audrey had loads to chat about. When I was preparing to write my book, *The Methodist Pentecost: 1758-1763*, John was the person who wrote the Foreword. They are still my friends and we talk about the things that occupy our attention and see each other from time to time.

The Revd. Irvine Grey still is my oldest friend and comes to see me every year. When I started preaching, I would often go Killadeas Methodist Church and Irvine was a small boy who used to attend with his mother. When we were in Uddingston he came to see us and when I was teaching at Nazarene Theological College, Manchester, he came to study for his MA. Right throughout the years he has been my friend and many a time Jeanne and I welcomed his visits. He was always interested in what I was reading and he wrote the Foreword to my book, *Epworth: The Cradle of Methodism.*

The Revd. Fred and Mrs. Cowan have always been friends since our days at Enniskillen Technical College and we often visited Methodist

Churches in our area. When I was about to start my second year in Hurlet Nazarene College, Fred joined us and we were together two years. We saw each other a lot and visited each other in our homes. When Jeanne and I were invited to the services in honour of our days at Nazarene Theological College in Didsbury in 2004, Fred was one of the invited guests. He loved coming to our home and we spent together many an hour reminiscing. While I was working on my book in 2014, *John Wesley: The Death of Christ*, he kindly wrote the Foreword. Fred and I go back a long way, almost sixty-three years, and it is a pleasure to welcome him whenever he comes this way.

Jeanne and I have known Bill and Lorraine Graham nearly forty-two years ago. When we first came to Manchester we worshipped sometimes at the Brooklands Church of the Nazarene and we got to know Bill and Lorraine. We have been good friends all these years and especially in the last five years they have been in our home many times. When we began the Wesley Fellowship, Bill and Lorraine joined and he was appointed Editor of The Wesley Fellowship Bulletin. Bill and I had something in common – we enjoyed books! When I published, *A Burning And A Shining Light: The Life and Ministry of William Bramwell*, 2009, Bill kindly supplied the Foreword. Later on, when I had published, *Dr. Adam Clarke: Methodist Preacher and Scholar*, in 2015, Bill again supplied the Foreword. All through forty-two years, Bill and Lorraine have been dear friends and were often in our home in Jeanne's last year. When attending Jeanne's funeral, Bill had carefully marked all her Christian values and spoke of her care for those that were around her and for all those whom she met. I count it a privilege to have known Bill and Lorraine above forty years.

We first met John and Pat when we went up to preach at the People's Mission, South Shields, in 2007. We stayed in their home and we met their boys. We stayed with them ten times and we visited the places round about. When I had the stroke ten years ago, I didn't want to travel and John and Pat visited us in Manchester. We enjoyed their company and called by phone to ask how they were.

Denzil and Marina McIlfatrick were friends of ours sixty years ago and I first met Denzil when he came and preached at Manoo Mission Hall. We chattered every time he came and that has gone over sixty years. He married Marina and every time we visited the Campmeeting they were both there. Denzil moved to Belfast and for ten years they have visited us two times a year. They are a wonderful couple and Denzil knows everything about the Lord's people!

There is one item that I would like to mention. All her life Jeanne has been a poet and during the years she was married, she loved to put her thoughts into poetry. At first she didn't want me to see what she had written and for many a year she kept them private. In Uddingston Church of the Nazarene she finally showed me what she had written and it was a revelation to me. After that she showed me her writings and down through fifty years, she got my text and wrote upon it herself. I was astounded at what she had written, sometimes following the text and at other times branching out on her own. She loved to write and one year she supplied her writings for us to put on our Christmas card. Poetry is a very special gift and Jeanne enjoyed what she was doing. Sometimes she followed the points I was making and added something to what I was saying. Now her writings are left behind and I get comfort by reading her poems. Jeanne contributed far more in writing and she leaves behind what God had given her.

Jeanne was a reader of books and from, *William Cooke on Entire Sanctification*, which I had published in 1978, and, *General William Booth*, published in 2016, twenty-four books in all, she read them all and encouraged me to write. For forty years she had seen my writing and she was prompting me to write further. In twenty-four books that I had written, she had plenty of time to read and the very first copy of every book I had written was first shown to Jeanne. There was one book that I never had written, *Through the Year with John and Charles Wesley*, and from time to time, she remembered that I had never tried to write about the Wesleys and she rebuked me for not trying! If our Lord will enable me to write, the next book will be on the Wesleys and Jeanne will have her wish granted!

Jeanne was with me fifty-five years and five months and in all that time I never heard her saying or doing anything that was wrong. She was a beloved wife, mother and grandmother and in all that time she was kind, loving and generous. She loved me, Keith and our sons, Stephen and Jonathan, and Jonathan's two children, Joe and Lucy. She was the loveliest woman any man could marry and in all her life with me we loved and cared for one another. Now that she has gone to heaven, I, together with my two sons and Keith and with our grandchildren, Joe and Lucy, miss her so much. I just keep praying that all my family will look back and see her quiet spirit and gentle nature and realize that she was born of God and filled with the Spirit.

Jeanne and I attended Brooklands Church of the Nazarene until the first Sunday in September, 2016, and she said that in the service she was not well. All of us concluded that she was better served with District Nurses coming in four times a day. The nurses were very kind and gentle and following lunch, she was allowed to sit in the chair in the dining room and go to bed at seven or eight. For five months this was her life but we could see that she became quiet and all of this time she was cared by me, Keith, Stephen and Jonathan, and her grandchildren, Joe and Lucy. Her last playing the piano was in December and this was eighty-four years after she had first started. All through January, 2017, she was attended by the nurses and we never left her. On February 4 she was a little worse and when the ambulance came, she was taken to Whythenshawe Hospital and all the night she was visited by a doctor or a nurse. On Sunday, at 7am, she had died. Immediately the hospital rang Keith and together with Stephen and Jonathan, we went for the last visit. She was transferred to a room and when we saw her, the body was not yet cold. She had died in the Lord and was promoted to glory.

On Friday, February 17, we arrived at the graveyard and met with both the Revd. Karl Standfield and the Revd. Colin Wood. She was taken out of the hearse and Keith, Stephen, Jonathan and Joe carried her to the grave. It was a beautiful morning and Karl officiated with great detail and the crowd stood around and sang her favourite hymn. Back at the college the chapel was full and Colin Wood was the officiating minister. There were four hymns that Jeanne had chosen and the singing was great and Mrs. Audrey Bolton, pianist, played the piano. The hymns were, 'With harps and with viols,' 'Have you any room for Jesus?', 'Sing the wonderous love of Jesus,' and, 'The Head that once was crowned with thorns.' The five tributes were brought with feeling: Keith Romig, Stephen McGonigle, Jonathan McGonigle, Bridget Wilkie and Bill Graham. Janice McGonigle contributed with, 'Great is Thy faithfulness' and the Revd. Colin Wood preached on I Corinthians 15:12-14.

But if it is preached that Christ has been raised from the dead, how come some of you say that there is no resurrection of the dead? If there is no resurrection of the dead, then not even Christ has been raised. And if Christ has not been raised, our preaching is useless and so is your faith.

It is customary for there to be an address or a eulogy in a service like this – even a full-blown sermon! And the instruction I was given was to 'preach.' I will be mindful of the time – and if Jeanne were here she's be saying ".... just get on with it and let these people have a cup of tea."

But there are some things I want to say. First to say that it is a great privilege to share in the service today. There are so many links and memories in this place and I feel a part of them. London, - Walthamstow and Battersea, Manchester – Church and College, and so on. And when – some months ago now – Herbert and Jeanne expressed their desire that I be involved in this service I was a bit taken aback but I felt, and feel, greatly honoured.

Well, **the first part of the sermon** is already before you. It is the life and testimony of the one we are remembering today. If you have not been moved and blessed and encouraged by the faith and faithfulness of Jeanne McGonigle, you must have a very insensitive heart, for she 'being dead yet speaketh.' And the life of service and prayer of this wife and mother is a lesson and example to us all. She knew God's love for her; Jesus Christ was her Lord and Saviour; she lived and died in the Faith – and we should do likewise. We are thanking God for every remembrance of our sister in Christ.

The **second part of the sermon** is here in this chapel ... this company ... of family, friends, colleagues, representatives of church congregations. And this company is all eloquent tribute to Jeanne's life and memory. And there are others unable to be here, who are part of this group and who have been blessed and encouraged by the life of Jeanne. We represent those on pilgrimage – marching to Zion! - the beautiful city of God. And as Charles Wesley puts it, "... part of His Host have crossed the flood and part are crossing now." Jeanne has arrived safely on the other shore.

We thank God for the blessing and encouragement of Jeanne's life. We thank God for the company of the redeemed and for the joy of being a part of the family of God.

The **next part of the sermon** – are some words from the Apostle Paul. In 1 Corinthians 15, Paul is talking about the resurrection – the resurrection of Christ and the resurrection of the dead. *"But if it preached that Christ has been raised from the dead, how come some of you say that there is no resurrection of the dead. If there is no resurrection of the dead, then not even Christ has been raised. And if Christ has not been raised, our preaching is useless and so is your faith."*

The interesting thing here is the way Paul chooses to handle this truth. Instead of coming at it in a positive way – and proclaiming the truth and the benefits of the resurrection, he uses this negative approach. He is, in effect, saying ... "What if?" He raises the question, "what if Christ has not been raised from the dead!" Verse 14, "If Christ has into been raised" ... what then? Well, he answers his own question.

1.   And first of all, **preachers would become redundant**. Verse 14 - "our preaching is useless." There'd be no good news to proclaim; we'd have services without sermons! If Christ is nor risen there's be no Message of Hope in a world that desperately needs hope. I don't know how many sermons Jeanne listed to over the years – quite a few, and not least from her preacher-husband, but I know she delighted in hearing the Preaching of the Word. As the old hymn puts it, "Tell me the stories of Jesus; write on my heart every word ..."

2.   No resurrection? Preachers would become redundant. Then Paul says, "**... and faith would become useless.**" Verse 17, *If there be no*

resurrection your faith is vain (… futile is the word in the AV). Not only would there be no message to proclaim, there would be no truth to believe.

Jeanne McGonigle was a woman of faith – the faith that is "sure of things hoped for and certain of things not seen!" But if there is no resurrection, faith is vain, futile and empty.

3. "What if – Christ be not risen?" No preaching. No faith …. Paul goes on, there would be **no forgiveness of sin**, *"if Christ be not risen you are still in your sins."*

Mrs C. F. Alexander wrote:
He died that we might be forgiveness
He died to make us good.

But if there is no resurrection, and sin and death claimed the victory, and the cross was the end, there would be no forgiveness, we would be without hope and without God in the world – but we used to sing at those great Easter Conventions in Battersea:
Death could not keep its prey
Jesus my Saviour
He tore the bars away
Jesus, my Lord.
… and, *Up from the grave He arose!*

Like so many here today, Jeanne McGonigle met the risen Saviour. She saw the marks of the nail-prints and the wound in His side. And like Thomas of old, confessed Jesus as Lord - "My Lord and My God" - and sins were forgiven and there was peace with God. But if Christ be nor risen we have no hope of forgiveness - "we are still in our sins."

4. No preaching. No Faith. No Forgiveness. Paul also says, if Christ be not risen, there is **no hope for the future** – there is no home in heaven; no eternal life. Verses 18-19: *If Christ has not been raised … then those also have fallen asleep in Christ are lost. If only for this life we have hope in Christ, then we are to be pitted more than all men.*

If Christ be not risen, if there were no resurrection, the note of celebration would be absent from this service. There are no mansions in glory, no place prepared for God's people, no great company in white robes gathered around the throne. They are gone, lost -annihilated. If Christ be nor risen no gift of eternal life, and we cannot say, with H. G. Spafford, "The sky not the grave is our goal."

BUT NOW! Paul takes the Gospel trumpet and puts it to his lips - he moves from the negative to the positive. *"But Christ has indeed been raised from the dead."* And we have something to preach about. We can put our faith in God. Forgiveness is available to all who repent and believe. And there is a land that is fairer then day. Our sister, Jeanne, is now with the Lord. Death has lost its sting; the grave has been robbed of its victory, and we say, thanks be to God who gives us the victory through our Lord Jesus Christ.

Now, the question is, do we rejoice in this truth? We have the example and blessing of Jeanne's life before us. What do you say to all this? The most fitting tribute that we could bring in memory and thanksgiving for Jeanne McGonigle's life is for each one to love the Saviour she loved, and follow and serve the Christ she served. And put our faith in the one who gave His life that we might be ransomed, healed, restored, forgiven! And if we were to do this, I know nothing would please Jeanne more, than to know that at this service in her memory someone put their faith in Christ and came to the Saviour for forgiveness and new life.

As we were singing, "Have you any room for Jesus?", for a day is coming when at the Name of Jesus every knee shall bow and every tongue confess that Jesus is Lord. Some will gladly and willingly – and the confession will be made with joy. But there will be those who will confess reluctantly – it will be a confession of judgement. And what they refused to do in this like, they will be forced to do on that great Day of the Lord. Let us confess Christ now! Today! ... and be a part of that group, who will confess Christ then - because they trusted Him now. Friends – but now is Christ risen! And because He lives we will live also.

The last addition was the anthem, 'The Lord bless thee and keep thee,' (Rutter). Jeanne wanted one of her poems to be read at the funeral and she chose, 'O, Saviour of mine.'

>O, Saviour of mine
>What a joy Thou art
>Thou hast filled my life
>Thou hast filled my heart
>O'ershadowed by grace
>O'erwhelmed with Thy love

My heart overflows
With a song from above
More joy will be mine
When I see Thy face
Radiant with glory
Transcended with grace.

Jeanne McGonigle, 1st October, 2005.

All of us then went to the cafe and for the next hour and a half, the talk was of Jeanne and how she had worshipped the Lord all her life.

It is now a year and a half since Jeanne was buried and we talk among ourselves what Jeanne had done throughout her days. Each day the family is here but when they are gone, it is me and my thoughts. Every day I miss her terribly and when I sit in the lounge, her smiling photograph looks down from the top of the piano. I know she has gone to be with her Lord and Saviour and all of us must miss her terribly and cling to the Lord and then at last 'we will dwell in the house of the Lord for ever.'

A funeral stone was ordered and the sculptor has written:

In loving memory
Jeanne Olive McGonigle
Born 30th July, 1921
Died 5th February, 2017
Beloved wife, mother and grandmother
Forever with the Lord

Tribute by Stephen

Music played an important part in Mum's life, and was integral to her role as a pastor's wife. This enabled a partnership whereby her husband preached and Mum provided the music which is such a dominant feature of worship within the Nazarene church.

There was always a piano within the home, and Mum would often play it for no other reason than for the sheer pleasure that it gave. She also loved to sing, and always enjoyed this aspect of a service. From her time as a young lady singing in the choir at the Billy Graham Crusades, through decades of church services and the changing fashions within music, both sacred and secular, Jeanne loved to learn new music and also to sing and play her favourites.

Mum learnt the piano as a child, along with her younger sister Pamela. She was taught at school which was a state school, as well as lessons at home. Forever modest about her abilities, Mum considered herself no more than an average pianist. This was in part a reflection of her dislike of being in the limelight. However, as a Pastor's wife and a church pianist, she considered it her role and duty to assist her husband. That does not mean to say that she performed these roles as a chore, indeed she felt blessed that she could indeed serve the Lord in this way and in partnership with her husband.

In reality, Mum was a more than proficient musician, and to be able to lead a congregation in the singing of hymns and choruses, is much more than simply playing the music as shown in a hymn book. Different occasions, and numbers within a congregation, call for subtle differences to which she was very much aware. If the tone of a service was devotional, it required a wholly different approach to that required when the service was bright and required boldly played hymns of praise. Her ability to play well by ear (without written music) was an especial gift. It would for instance be quite usual for a request to be made for a chorus, and there to be no music to hand. Mum had the ability to play it in any case. Above all, she knew how important the aspect of communal singing was to a service and what a joyous activity it was.

Her great love was for the canon of hymns from over the ages. She owned many hymnals, and in particular used the Redemption Hymnal. We still have her much used copy, covered in brown paper and then covered in cellophane. This accompanied Mum wherever she went if she was likely to be required to play. Her knowledge of hymns was truly encyclopaedic, the legacy of her many years of devoted service. There were numerous occasions whereby she would advise her husband as to which hymns would be complementary to the theme of his sermon, and that he in turn found her advice invaluable. She knew which hymns could be sung to alternative tunes, and this was based on her realisation that praise through song was every bit as important as other aspects of a service.

Her knowledge was coupled with a genuine love for the poetry contained within many hymns. Mum was someone who had in any case a great love of the spoken word, and would often recite a huge amount of poetry from memory. It was an ability which resulted in much gentle teasing on the part of her family, who knew that, if given the appropriate prompt, she would launch into a recitation whether it was wanted or not! In reality, this ability was much admired by all of her family, especially as much of what she'd recite had been learnt as a young girl in the 1920s.

Although Mum loved all sacred music, it was the traditional hymns which she loved the best. These hymns had a gravitas and majesty to which she instinctively responded. She also had a particular love of Handle's 'Messiah', which she regarded as having been written as the result of Divine inspiration. She sang it on several occasions and went to see performances of this piece on many more. It was a piece of which she never tired. Some of the more modern examples of sacred music, she regarded with less favour, finding them strangely repetitive in terms of melodic progression and how the words scanned. She also found that some of the words to modern choruses where somewhat banal and 'dumbed down', lacking the clear sighted, evident and worshipful tone found in the traditional hymns.

This doesn't mean that she dismissed all modern sacred music. Far from it, indeed she loved to learn a new chorus or song which she would hear. Mum had a particular fondness for choruses which were written in what she considered a 'Yiddish style' consisting usually of a quick tempo and invariably played in a minor key.

Apart from sacred music, Mum had a lifelong love of classical music, and in particular Chopin and Beethoven. She considered Chopin's piano music to be the greatest ever to be written for that instrument. Beethoven was her absolute ideal when it came to orchestral music, and she loved his compositions. She had a collection of recorded music which ranged from 78 records, through LPs, audio cassettes and finally CDs. The car radio was always tuned to the classical music stations as were various radios throughout the home. As her mobility was reduced and her eyesight diminished in later years, she grew to listen ever more to broadcast music.

Her love of music was therefore a constant throughout Mum's long and productive life. It mattered little from where it originated, what made her love a piece of music could be boiled down to three elements, that it was tuneful, melodic and 'made sense'. She very much admired the music of Lennon and McCartney for instance, even if she considered their lifestyles were in opposition to her faith. She enjoyed pieces from popular musicals and had been often known to write Christian words to what was originally a secular tune. She did indeed believe in the statement, 'Why should the devil have all the best music?'

Tribute by Jonathan

Recently Dad has started his autobiography and he asked me to write a piece on Mum as a mum.

When Mum passed away on Feb 5th 2017 at the age of 95 after a fairly short period of illness, the lives of myself and brothers Stephen and Keith, and of course, Dad, changed immeasurably. That rock, that female influence was no longer around, and we found ourselves suddenly without that familiar face and voice that we had known and loved for all our lives.

Mum (and we rarely called her mother except in jest) was exactly that – a mum who stayed at home most of her life to bring up her 3 sons and to provide a solid home life for us and Dad. She chose not to pursue a career as she saw it as her duty as a wife and mother to be the homemaker and she certainly did that. Indeed, she willingly moved from London, to Glasgow then Leeds and finally Manchester as dad moved between churches and the Nazarene college. Although at times finances were tight we never went short of food or clothing or any essentials as mum kept a close eye on money and an even closer eye on the local shops where a bargain or a deal were to be had!.

Her love of music has already been commented on but music did play a huge part in mum's life be it church music or classical music with Beethoven being her particular favourite. She was also a poetry lover and, in her earlier days, an extensive reader, to the extent that we always claimed that whatever the situation mum could quote a line of poetry or a verse from a hymn that would be appropriate.

Mum also loved words – whether it was working out the Latin roots of particular words, working on crosswords or playing Scrabble with the family on a Sunday afternoon, mum was in her element. A TV favourite of mum's was Countdown which she watched from the early days. She once wrote to the host, Richard Whiteley, explaining her two-year old grandson, Joe, had learned his numbers and letters from watching his show and he read the letter out some weeks later. Some 18 years later Joe appeared on Countdown and reached the semi-final and mum was very proud.

Mum was also very pleased to firstly welcome Janice into the family when she married Steve and then also Carolyn when she married myself. She was also delighted to become a grandmother in 1992 and again in 1996 when Joe and Lucy were born and she took great delight in looking after them when the need arose and then watching them grow into the adults they became. Mum was loving and caring, she always had time for people and never had a bad word to say about anyone. She certainly was no pushover though as we all found out from time to time as she ensured our chores were done and our school homework was completed.

Finally, I cannot finish this without talking about the guiding force in mum's life which was her faith in God. Mum was a truly committed born-again Christian and her faith led her every day of her life. Her love of God never wavered even through the trials and tribulations of everyday life and she never doubted her faith. I know that mum is now with God and is at peace.

To everyone else she was Jeanne or Mrs McGonigle but to us she was simply, Mum. Truly loved and dearly missed.

Books by Revd Dr Herbert Boyd McGonigle

William Cooke on Entire Sanctification, Beacon Hill Press, Kansas City, Missouri, 1978.

The Arminianism of John Wesley, Moorleys Print & Publishing, Ilkeston, Derbyshire, 1988.

John Wesley and the Moravians, Moorleys Print & Publishing, Ilkeston, Derbyshire, 1995.

John Wesley's Doctrine of Prevenient Grace, Moorleys Print & Publishing, Ilkeston, Derbyshire, 1995.

Scriptural Holiness: The Wesleyan Distinctive, Moorleys Print & Publishing, Ilkeston, Derbyshire, 1995.

Sufficient Saving Grace: John Wesley's Evangelical Arminianism, 350 pages, Paternoster Publishing, Carlisle, Cumbria, 2001.

To God Be The Glory: The Killadeas Convention 1952-2002, Moorleys Print & Publishing, Ilkeston, Derbyshire, 2002.

John Wesley's Arminian Theology: An Introduction, Moorleys Print & Publishing, Ilkeston, Derbyshire, 2005.

A Burning and a Shining Light: The Life and Ministry of William Bramwell, Moorleys Print & Publishing, Ilkeston, Derbyshire, 2009.

Christianity or Deism? John Wesley's Response to John Taylor's Denial of the Doctrine of Original Sin, Moorleys Print & Publishing, Ilkeston, Derbyshire, 2012.

John Wesley: Exemplar of the Catholic Spirit, Moorleys Print & Publishing, Ilkeston, Derbyshire, 2014.

Charles Wesley: For All, For All My Saviour Died, Moorleys Print & Publishing, Ilkeston, Derbyshire, 2014.

John Wesley: The Death of Christ, Moorleys Print & Publishing, Ilkeston, Derbyshire, 2014.

Epworth: The Cradle of Methodism, Moorleys Print & Publishing, Ilkeston, Derbyshire, 2014.

John Wesley: Doctrine of Final Judgement, Moorleys Print & Publishing, Ilkeston, Derbyshire, 2015.

Thomas Walsh: Saint and Scholar, Moorleys Print & Publishing, Ilkeston, Derbyshire, 2015.

Our Story: Autobiographical thoughts from the pen of Revd. Dr. Herbert B. McGonigle, Nazarene Theological College Archives, Manchester, 2015.

Dr. Adam Clarke: Methodist Preacher and Scholar, Moorleys Print & Publishing, Ilkeston, Derbyshire, 2015.

Gideon Ouseley: Methodist Preacher and Biblical Scholar, Moorleys Print & Publishing, Ilkeston, Derbyshire, 2015.

Thomas Cook: Evangelist and Saint, Moorleys Print & Publishing, Ilkeston, Derbyshire, 2016.

The Methodist Pentecost, 1758-1763, Moorleys Print & Publishing, Ilkeston, Derbyshire, 2016.

John Fletcher, Methodist Saint and Scholar, Moorleys Print & Publishing, Ilkeston, Derbyshire, 2016.

An Appreciation of Revd. Dr. John Henry Jowett's Heaven's Hallelujah, Moorleys Print & Publishing, Ilkeston, Derbyshire, 2016.

General William Booth, Moorleys Print & Publishing, Ilkeston, Derbyshire, 2016.

John Wesley on The Great Salvation, Moorleys Print & Publishing, Ilkeston, Derbyshire, 2017.

Samuel Chadwick: Preacher and Evangelist, Moorleys Print & Publishing, Ilkeston, Derbyshire, 2017.

Francis William Crossley, Moorleys Print & Publishing, Ilkeston, Derbyshire, 2018.

Dr. Alexander Maclaren: Preacher and Expositor, Moorleys Print & Publishing, Ilkeston, Derbyshire, 2018.